Filled up Full

Written and illustrated by Joy V. Dueland

The Christian Science Publishing Society
Boston, Massachusetts, U. S. A.

Parents' Letter

Recognizing thoughts from God is a joyful experience and an important lesson for children.

Filled Up Full helps children discern the thoughts that come from God as those that bring joy, strength, kindness, selflessness, honesty, happiness, and goodness to their lives and to others. It helps them see that when they are filled up full with God's thoughts, there is no room for anything unlike God.

Jesus says, "Take heed therefore that the light which is in thee be not darkness. If thy whole body therefore be full of light, having no part dark, the whole shall be full of light, as when the bright shining of a candle doth give thee light" (Luke 11:35, 36).

Children can learn that when they have a single-minded focus on Godlike thoughts, their lives are filled with this light of good.

G50316

©1974 The Christian Science Publishing Society
All rights reserved
ISBN 0-87510-386-3
Printed in the United States of America

Who do you see?

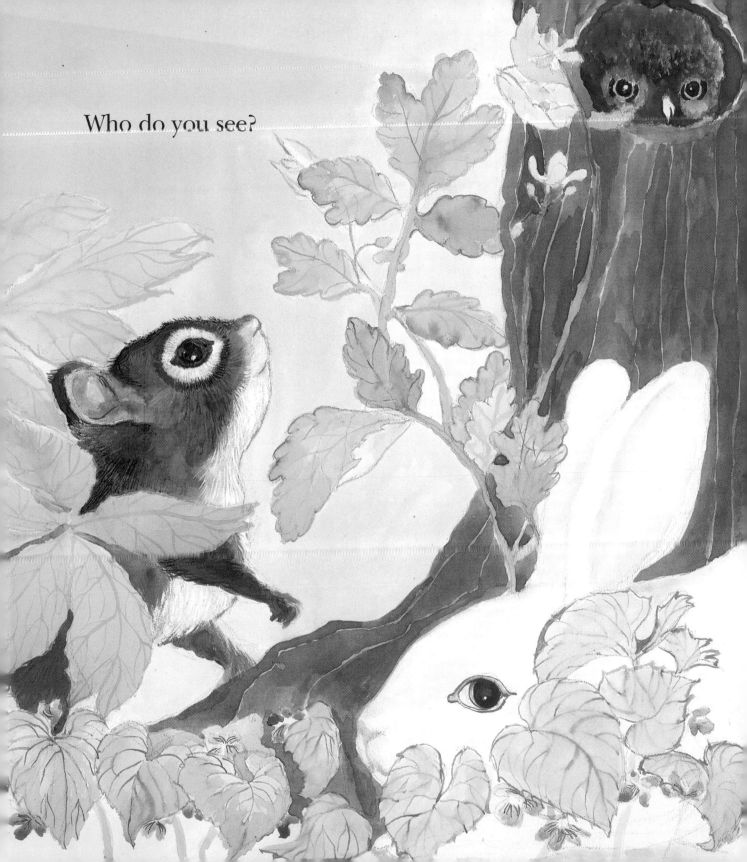

See this kitten?

She thinks only kitten thoughts.
She doesn't think of wading like a duck.

She wouldn't crawl like a turtle.
Because she's a kitten
  —filled up full with kitten thoughts!

See this rabbit?
He thinks only rabbit thoughts.

He doesn't think of swinging like a monkey.

He wouldn't wiggle like a worm in a hole.

Because he's a rabbit
   —filled up full with rabbit thoughts!

See this squirrel?

He thinks only squirrel thoughts.

He doesn't think of swimming like a fish.

He doesn't want to hoot like an owl.

Because he's a squirrel
—filled up full with squirrel thoughts!

See me?
I'm filled up full with thoughts from God.

So there's no room for grouchy thoughts,
or even little mean thoughts,

God's truth makes me strong.
God's love makes me kind.

I'm filled up full
with thoughts from God.

See me?
I'm filled up full
with thoughts from God.

So I wouldn't think of being selfish,
or telling even a little lie.

God's love makes me share.
God's truth makes me honest.
I'm filled up full with thoughts from God.

See me?
I'm filled up full with thoughts from God.

So I wouldn't think of being sad,
or being even a little bad.

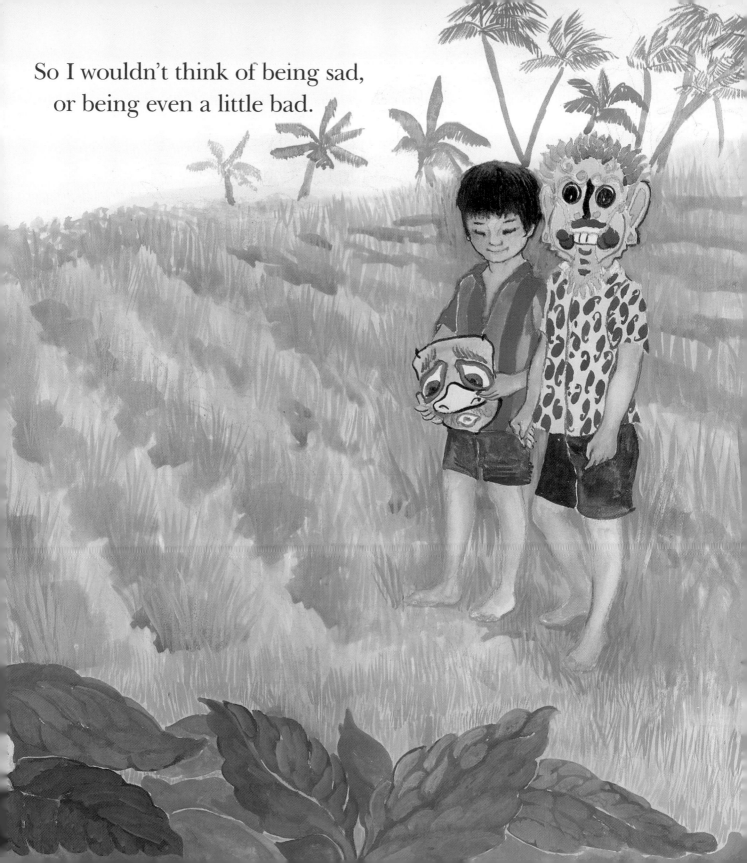

God's love makes me happy.
God's truth makes me good.
I'm filled up full with thoughts from God.

See us?

God fills us all —

full up!